Spiritual Letters
Series 1-5

Spiritual Letters
(Series 1-5)

David Miller

For Brian

all good
wishes
David

chax 2011

ISBN 978 0 925904 98 0

Also by David Miller:

The Caryatids, Enitharmon Press, London, 1975
South London Mix, Gaberbocchus Press, London, 1975
Malcolm Lowry and the Voyage that Never Ends, Enitharmon
            Press, 1976
Primavera, Burning Deck Press, Providence, RI, 1979
Unity, Singing Horse Press, Blue Bell, PA, 1981
Losing to Compassion, Origin Press, Kyoto, 1985
W.H. Hudson and the Elusive Paradise, Macmillan,
            London / St. Martins Press, NY, 1990
Pictures of Mercy: Selected Poems, Stride, Exeter, 1991
Stromata, Burning Deck Press, 1995
Collected Poems, University of Salzburg Press, Salzburg, 1997
Art and Disclosure: Seven Essays, Stride, 1998
The Waters of Marah: Selected Prose 1973-1995, Singing
            Horse Press, Philadelphia, 2003 /
            Shearsman Books, Exeter, 2005
Spiritual Letters (I-II) and other writings, Reality Street
            Editions, Hastings, 2004

The Dorothy and Benno Stories, Reality Street Editions, 2005
British Poetry Magazines 1914-2000: A History and Bibliography of 'Little Magazines' (with Richard Price), The British Library, London / Oak Knoll Press, Newcastle, DE, 2006
In the Shop of Nothing: New and Selected Poems, Harbor Mountain Press, Brownsville, VT, 2007

Edited by David Miller:

A Curious Architecture: a selection of contemporary prose poems (with Rupert Loydell), Stride, 1996
The ABCs of Robert Lax (with Nicholas Zurbrugg), Stride, 1999
Music while drowning: German Expressionist Poems (with Stephen Watts), Tate Publishing, London, 2003
The Lariat and other writings by Jaime de Angulo, Counterpoint, Berkeley, 2009

Acknowledgements:

These texts were first published in *Across Borders, Bongos of the Lord, Delicate Iron, Fire, First Intensity, Free Verse, Gangway, Golden Handcuffs Review, Hassle, House Organ, Intimacy, kadar koli, Kater Murr's Press, Lamport Court, Metre, NOON: Journal of the Short Poem, Oasis, Painted, spoken, Poetry Salzburg Review, Sentence: a Journal of Prose Poetics, Shadow Train, Shearsman, Shuffle Boil, Southfields, 26, Versal* and *Vértebra: Revista de Artes, Literatura y Crítica* (with translations by Fernando Pérez), as well as in *A Gathering for Gael Turnbull*, ed. Peter McCarey, Au Quai (Glasgow and Staines, Middlesex), *In the Company of Poets*, ed. John Rety, Hearing Eye (London), *poetry tREnD: Eine englisch-deutsche Anthologie zeitgenössischer Lyrik*, ed. Aprilia Zank (with translations by Judith Königer, Sabine Stiglmayr, Julia Offermann and Anna Hubrich), Lit Verlag (Berlin) and *Take Five 06*, ed. John Lucas, Shoestring Press (Nottingham, UK).

Various parts of this book have also appeared in the following limited edition publications: *Spiritual Letters (1-7)*, tel-let (Charleston, Illinois); *Spiritual Letters (1-10)*, EMH Arts/Eagle Graphics (London), with artwork by Andrew Bick; *Spiritual Letters (1-12)*, hawkhaven press (San Francisco); *Spiritual Letters (Series 2, #1-5)*, Nyxpress (Sydney), with artwork by Denis Mizzi; *Spiritual Letters (Series 3, #1-7)*, Nyxpress, with artwork by Denis Mizzi; *Spiritual Letters (Series 4)*, hawkhaven press, with artwork by Louise Victor; and *Spiritual Letters (Series 5)*, Nyxpress. The first two series were published in *Spiritual Letters (I-II) and other writings*, Reality Street Editions (Hastings), and *Spiritual Letters (Series 3)* appeared from Stride Publications in Exeter.

To relieve confusion, the sections that were published by tel-let and EMH Arts/Eagle Graphics, as well as *Spiritual Letters (1-12)* (hawkhaven), were all from the first series of the project — I simply wasn't thinking of it as consisting of separate series at the time.

I would like to acknowledge the feedback and encouragement of various friends over the years... no real point in listing them, though, as they know who they are. I would also like to thank Charles Alexander for making this publication possible, and Cynthia Miller for providing the cover artwork.

Contents:

Spiritual Letters (Series I-5)

Spiritual Letters (Series I: I-I5)   I3
Spiritual Letters (Series 2: I-5)   3I
Spiritual Letters (Series 3: I-I2)   39
Spiritual Letters (Series 4: I-I2)   55
Spiritual Letters (Series 5: I-5)   73

Notes   95

Spiritual Letters
(Series I)

For an end, a constant ending: images from a life counterpoised with imageless reflections. Smoke rises, spreads over roofs. In the room a sparrow huddles against the wall, near books and china. We discuss the transcendent and the satirical, and find ourselves wondering: a novel? The sheets of paper blacken. Burning animals amongst burning trees haunted the child. You cannot get from A to B by walking a line from one to the other. The girl's eyes habituated to begging touch your lips, burning them. Memory's blasted. He'll keep a record of the epiphany in his breast pocket, if not sewn into the lining of his coat.

The woman has entered through the doorway, a metal cup in her hand; her face, through the thin veil, is that of someone still very young and unwilling to believe in her beauty. A caption reads "Sacraments" and pertains to the act of blessing taking place in the foreground. In front of the underground station a little girl pisses in the gutter, while her mother holds her hand. You leap high in the air; the leap is held through categories of pain. Bruises and welts beneath your clothing. Nights when there has been no one you would call to your aid. I remember a taxicab ride at night in a downpour, when someone got into the cab beside you and all sense of protection failed. The predicament: as if having fallen into it, I found I could do nothing at all. A silence that harms; an absence of writing that calls for an outpouring.

...letter by letter. Having no wish to be detained by clever fabrications, stories that might distract. A dark courtyard, a lecture on aesthetics. — And if art is only lies, for the sake of rapture and power? Facing the wall, away from the wind, she struck a match for her cigarette — the flame drawing my look. Feckless, volatile girl; in the dream she began shouting at me as I turned away from her. — Flung across the hospital room by the Holy Ghost, the musician said. A phone-call: the driver survived; he died — the friend I'd stopped seeing. I thought of how he'd insisted on reading poem after poem to me at dinner; I'd looked (but not wanting to) at the spittle ejected upon his lip as he spoke the words. Faces of friends by my bed. Memory's unquenched: her long hair that she tossed around her neck; her hand that reached for mine. *Eye toward eye....* Slow phleboclysis (drop by drop; into the vein).

A white-haired rationalist in a pin-stripe suit, rolling around on the floor; his much-lined face contorted as he cracks jokes about the "hind-parts" of God. — How odd, how *very* funny, he laughs at the idea of a revealing of something that yet remains hidden. The little girl sat looking at the brightly colored pages of a comic book. The scrub ablaze. A group of children arrived stark naked to hear stories which clustered around the words *poor, pure* and *merciful*. Having come to the wall he poses standing on the stones.

.

the words dark
inescapable
an intervention
(by something
or someone)
on a stone
by the path

An old man fell down in the street; another man helped him up, comforting him, then suddenly began shouting abuse both at the old man and at passers-by. Pierced; wordless. — Love is the *exceptional* thing, he said; I knew he meant sexual love. You could locate her by her youth as much as her beauty or her violent moods in which she excoriated at length each of your traits. Revealing the cuts on her arms. A fruitless vine. The girls walked past us through the grasses, laughing; we were crouching down, looking at an image of an elephant figured on the stone. — You couldn't mention mythology in that house without feeling remorse. Nothing except for its own sake. Brick and earthen mound, metal plate and token accoutrements: these become an allegory of divine judgment. He was lying in bed with his mouth full of blood when he heard someone at the other end of the room shouting out: That man in the blue pajamas, I know him! To find himself in a hospital ward with an art critic was bad enough, he thought; but the man started telling him how much he'd admired his last show, and he was helpless in the face of it.

Lost in a once familiar area, wet from the drizzle, I moved toward the lights of a string of late night shops, following behind a small group of teenagers. In the dream, a song with the words *Life can be tough when you get stuck in the butter* played on the café radio, while the waitress' cat rolled around in the butter dish. Children from my own childhood, rows of faces bereft of speech. Rain and street noise; static. A stray description: enclosed by aesthetics, the ideas and beliefs disappeared into a play of sense perceptions. No inbeing, to your eyes; nothing to address save a set of gestures, moves, analogous to your own. — Dear, I said; oh my dear. The drawings on gelatin silver prints were an intervention, he said, provoked by illness. An imagined flight, ghostly and literal. Confronted by silence, the fantasies born of disillusionment are maddened and proliferate further.

A letter written within the shape of a hand. He arrived at the party with his wife, his head covered in bandages. Late in the evening she slowly removed the swathes, seemingly oblivious of the people around them. From the years spent in distant travel, a long series of paintings depicting flowers. Messages disguised as postage stamps. In a dream, the image of the crimson snow plant. He told the woman about a suicide attempt, before realising that she cultivated a flair for lapidation. Momently aware, and removed from shame by her rapture. It was my belief that I had a novel to write; I found myself with a handful of fragments. An absence of explanation. I had thought to speak of struggle but spoke of vigilance instead.

— You can't call any writing that's not concerned with drug-taking contemporary, someone said. — The analogy being a mirror...? — Are you who I think you are? he asked, and mentioned my name. —No, I replied, I'm somebody else. The long process of revision appealed to me with its possibilities of erasure and reversal. A layering of memories and images. A hand touching, a finger traveling along the line of affection. Late; voices loud, in the heat. No form of rhetoric could be adequate to what needs to be said, one to another. Drawn from her face, as we talked: an edge splendent in the obscurity. Unbearable to recall.

They invited me to join them in making art in collaboration, and I set to work enthusiastically. Holes drilled in wood, marks made on paper and canvas, writings arranged in patterns. Nights we spent sitting on the rooftop. The body had been laid out amongst clusters of brooches, pins. A lament for love, *Deep Song*, ends then begins again. He found himself progressively losing interest in the painting he'd once wanted to purchase, as the artist reworked it over several years. Recognition fails. A dream apart from the allure of confusion. A figure of stars seen waking through a glass wall.

A cold night wind. We talked together, upon the road leading from the house to the hills beyond.

> disrupted lines
> in clusters
> erratic shapes
> of tree branches
> how I trusted
> a cynosure
> brief comfort

The artist warned his students that he would mark them harshly for sham, evasion and insincerity. But it's sorrow that's provoked by thraldom. — Only the words of the text, you said, the reflection that appears in the mirror: nothing more. These were taken as realia: the child staring into the oil spread over a polished surface; the shapes that appear to his eyes; the onlookers who see nothing that he sees. For the sake of what one kind of writing fails to disclose, I attempt a writing of a different order; but each occasion's embedded in uncertainty. Gazing — finally — upon the images on a veil formed from blue flame.

Scribbled in the margins of the text: a confession. A girl runs past at the edge of your vision and all else that you see fails. We left the bar at three in the morning, having spent the evening getting drunk with a trauma nurse in a black floppy hat. I walked along the street with the little girl, holding her hand. The dream's a window through which you see the hurt changing her features. It was already morning when I was shifted into the ward. In vain I pulled the sheet over my head. After the crash in which his son was killed and he'd been trapped for hours in the wrecked car, he had gone wandering. Lost; turned away from what had been familiar. Eyes closed, she sang one melancholy song then another, the party at her café table falling silent to listen. The stone's to be inscribed or painted upon, not eaten.

He arrived at the door at five in the morning, with an expectation of some desperate action on your part. — *I'm not angry,* he said in an angry voice when you stood there unharmed. A landscape of reddish hues, hard by the sea. Inscribe in outline a dwelling, a tomb — a city of dwellings and tombs. The bones of a sparrow or mouse beneath the decorations and charms; the charred bones of a small child. As you walk along the littoral, the movements of your gaze *may result in unexpected 'wipes' of color.* A letter that answers accusations: unsent, it's kept in a cupboard, its eyes open in the dark. You retrace the confidences, too: the beatings her first lover gave her for his pleasure, his rejection of her when she was pregnant by him. Gainsay a concern with persuasion or display, elegance or finesse, as well as the formulas of ruin. Place another sheet alongside the first: move across, reflecting upon, engaging with, in places cancelling. An amateur, I write, rewrite — for the sake of what remains invisible in the showing-forth.

Open the book, flip through the pages: the frog turns into a devouring monster and back into a frog. — Dear (dead) friends, I am writing to you once more. *Dream geometry*, drawn, threaded. If I dream of him lending me books, I am led to that memory of how he would give books to a homeless young man who sat knitting in the town square. In an assemblage: old furniture; cardboard in rolls and sheets cut to shape; used light-bulbs; coverings of gold and silver foil. — A supernal throne, the man said. Chart whatever inversions, transformations you find. A script, cryptic, enigmatic, covers the pages of a notebook, spills over onto the assemblage. He turns away, addressing the absent and the dead. — It is my weakness, he says, that I exult in. Mercy following mercy.

You were walking in the gardens, with the notes beginning to sound. Your life: say it's all there, *as in a piece of arras work.* The old woman stopped the young stranger on the street and asked him to marry her. He stayed and talked with her, then went on his way. — If you wake up and see someone sitting bolt upright, don't worry, it'll be me. An architect who works with shards. One child stops and looks back in greeting, as the others run past. In the dark street, a handkerchief flapping from a door. For loss: these dissonances between the voices, *howling in seconds,* gravely performed. Who would mimic lamentations, mocking them? He was given a coat — to appease the dream in which he killed the man he called *a predacious shit.* — The gold surface was covered with writing, front and back. Contrite in spirit, broken, you cannot continue. Yearning for an old friend, by river, lake or lagoon. Playing improvisations late at night, I fell asleep and woke in the early hours, my clarinet beside me.

Waking to bruises on my right arm one morning, my left arm the next. *It's your ghost — not your immortal spirit — that's careering around, playing havoc. A ghost that doesn't require any death for it to be let loose.* The mules in their panic ran into the plum bushes and were caught fast. — You also allowed the archive to vanish! he said at the end of the objurgation. When she was asked to write about a famous author, my friend said: I could tell you my thoughts about him on a postcard. The artist paints the woman's name on a canvas, a brief phrase about her; he paints a phrase from her writings on another canvas. A large man in shirt sleeves hoses down the steps of the church. Texts on panels adorned the walls. Two small chairs facing the tree.

Spiritual Letters
(Series 2)

Everywhere we went, people had moved chairs and even beds out onto the pavement. Sea's redress; a releasing, he said. For your sake, you asked me to remember, speak, dream; what else could I do? The narratives are interrelated — the thread is pulled through one and then into another. Even if the people live remote from each other; or the events take place in different periods. A multitude, or you and I. I was offered wine by a young woman in the dream, and then woke. He had written, What purpose could there be for the memories that I have of those I've loved and who are dead or otherwise lost to me, if we were not to meet again? Saying the words back to him (and writing them) as far as I remember them.

We walked together through dark fields of tall grass. Talking to hear him talk, to follow where his thoughts might take us; talking to ease all the lost years in our friendship. In the quiet, you pointed out the inscriptions on the gilded panels. Remembering: pieces of glass within each iron ring in the column, colored and worked into relationship. Is it a disquisition that I should write? Again, I draw or paint over the words, leaving some visible, obscuring or cancelling others. The poet lines up his drinks on the table, sufficient to last him through the reading. He sits in the room next door to his listeners; they cup their ears to the wall, straining to catch his words. — *Ill-starred*, she said, the hour in which accidents fall to us and damage follows. In the hospital he imagines a letter that's delivered in spite of disaster; and he makes a likeness, the envelope's triangular stain hinting just barely at storm or flood or wreck. As an image of weeping: *tissues suspended from beneath the table.* — A room set aside for counselling, you said.

...that we may testify, not contrive. Night; a shelter: unseen, unheard. — What I am, is in relation, he said; what I become, in a shared inherence. *In a death, in weakness, inactivity, negation.* You wanted to describe everything, you said. Notebooks held within open hands. Divagations; kisses. We sat on a bench beside the pond, mallards and Canada geese nearby. A chapel on a hill overlooking the ruins of a temple: smoke-darkened ceiling, damaged frescoes. A young girl holds a rabbit, wrapped in the folds of her dress. A darkened room: a scribble of red, hypnagogic; pulsating, glowing, hovering over the pile of letters and photographs. I was pulled under the table where the others already crouched, while ornaments fell from the shaking walls and shattered. Despite every misfortune, the music — an elaboration of individual sounds, an unfolding or drawing-out from an interior — arrives. A night sleeping (trying to sleep) on the deck of the ship, against the engine's beat; waking over and again to wind, cold, sea spray. By the quayside, the street musician flutter-tongues on flute. Children listen to a story told in shadows.

We sat on a stone wall, taking turns drinking ouzo from the bottle's cap, while waiting for the ship to dock. A chair strapped to her back. Sleeping with difficulty; waking with difficulty in the mornings: you asked me to help by telephoning every day. You woke one morning and wrote a postcard to tell me: in the dream you were working on a large painting, surrounded by flying fish.

> alabaster
> in thin sheets
> framework
> of iron
> door posts inscribed
> smeared I can't
> locate again
> occluded
> the juncture
> the black
> diagonals

...walking away from me, abruptly, in the street at night. Jars broken in performance, an image of judgment. And the water — changing color, what did it become? On the tape, a voice striking off the minutes while the interrogation proceeded. The woman recorded that she'd written an account of her grief and then destroyed the pages.

— Anastasis, they queried; the name of a goddess? False stories were put into play. *Bicycling through the city, with his ears painted red.* — I was seduced, seduced myself, into living through illusion. —What would that mean? I asked. I put little credence in the story that he buried some of his writings in a tin can in a corner of the schoolhouse. Sleeping under mounds of white netting strung over the bed. Night, the shadow of a tree on the pavement — leaves moving in wind. By his own admission: a painter of blue puddles. He wanted to learn ancient Greek so that after his death he could converse with Heraclitus, Socrates and Plato. Each page of the stolen thesis was retrieved from the river, then taken home and ironed. Lines and patterns of dots, in wax on cloth; color in abeyance. Reflected: you and I together in your room, while you painted. Sitting on the sand near the quay, surrounded by geese. He asked us to look away when he rose from his sickbed and went to the bathroom. When we heard a knock we said: Come in; and the visitor who came in saw us sitting huddled together, our eyes still averted, and left without a word. A gathering-up of stray thoughts by a potlatch thinker, or so it was rumored. Marble or limestone slab, doorjamb or lintel. Finger or eye tracing what remains, what's shown.

Spiritual Letters
(Series 3)

Fountains splashed below as I crossed the walkways. A bed, strip-like against the wall. *Hide-and-go-seek.* Moving through level after level of the all but empty building.

> night
> a hand turning
> through a full circle
> hands
> coinciding
> her hand raised
> in reflection

A cloth ready for dyeing, lines etched into the waxed surface. Retelling the story to myself, recalling the details: a face, in lamplight; a shadow traced on the wall.... Earlier, waiting in the doorway... a storm of hail pounding the cobbled alley.

Sitting at a small table on the balcony, drinking wine and writing draft after draft by lamplight. More and more incapacitated, his head snapping backwards in spite of himself, the boy was stranded in the waiting room. Having dropped the heap of leaves, the little girl beseeched her sister and parents to help her pick them up again. — You should try writing a novel, he told me. *Dear is the honie that is lickt out of thornes.* Desire's thrown into confusion; overwhelmed. Full moon above trees in the long window. Stepping down — plunging into water. The stranger he'd been gazing at earlier suddenly came over to speak to him and then fetched a nurse, insisting he should be looked after immediately; her compassion caught him, so unexpected.

To be sung: *...that the lost might life inherit...* A sheet draped over the chair. We sat at a table between two banana plants, a pool of water gathering underneath. A banner of flame in the night sky, above the treetops and streetlights. In a shop on the way to her home, she chose a circular mirror for me to purchase; in another shop, fuchsias for herself. I dreamt that the artist — most famously narcissistic of her generation — had died; yet later in the dream I encountered her at a private view. The old woman turns a radio on at the back of the lecture hall, loud static interrupting the discussion. He arrived at my door, his suitcase full of fish bones. On the far wall of the living room, a sheet was draped around the mirror. Between the twin rocks, a reddish light — as if scumbled over the pond's surface. — *A good amulet*, he said, invoking, gathering protection. The small silver hand was engraved with letters, signs. — The motherfuckers won't let me sing, the woman said at her friend's funeral. Around the frame, a pattern of stars, or the names of angels.

The father and mother sat on their front steps, while out in the street their children played a game with a ball. It was my first visit and I had arrived in the early hours, the airport almost deserted; a drunken young cowboy in Stetson, chaps and spurred boots was singing *The Streets of Laredo* at the top of his voice. Pieces of paper, messages, were threaded through the boxes that the boy made after the woman's death. Having chased the cat away, he crouched down, talking gently to the frog in the corner of the room, reassuring it. — Could it have been a scholar in a former life, remiss in religious observances? In the dream there were two houses, the second a mirror image of the first, and it was in this second house, this reflection, that I thought I might live. He was asked if the recurrent black rectangle in his paintings was a symbol of himself. At a table in the cool night air, we were discussing the Greek poet whose grave my friend had visited. Two roosters perched on the wall by the outdoor toilet. *There were bush-fires here... nearby,* my friend wrote; *black ash blowing through the window and settling on the final proofs as I was reading them.*

The house on the mountain, above the temples, had become haunted... but also, he said, *far too draughty to rent.* Homeless men wrapped in blankets, sleeping or sitting hunched over in the pews. A man walked into the hall with a cat on his shoulder. Waking in the night, he looked through the doorway and saw his friend sitting in the other room, writing; waking again, he saw his friend asleep at his desk; and waking a third time, he looked in at his friend writing once more. — Columbaria, he said, for the thoughts and words, attaching, detaching themselves from the rows of spaces.

> *withdrawn*
> the roses
> the drumming
> rigid sync-
> opations
> the door
> of silver
> the faces
> the tears
> *withdrawn*
> the tears
> the gnashing
> of teeth

On the way to the sea we drove past a line of shanty dwellings, dwarfed by the houses that surrounded them. She was afraid that what she'd written was *the*

wreckage of empty description. A frenzy: gulls following
in the ship's wake out of the harbor.

Heavy rain falling on the table and chairs, the potted plants and flowers, the long grass and boards. Two magpies and a crow, moving back and forth through the leaves of the trees. He received in the mail a map of a city area, without any notations or accompanying letter. Black outlines of tar, rectangular: glistening on the pavement. A fragment of bone in a white cup on the table. He woke in pain, in a strange room; glancing in the bedside mirror, he saw that his face was bruised and streaked with blood. Someone writes on the stones, another taps on them with a stick. When my friend and I visited the old poet, he told us of what he'd seen during the war, what he'd gone through. I was writing a poem in his honor — drafting a second version — when the ringing of the phone woke me. She had hung sheets of black plastic over the shelves, covering all of the books.

– He recognised the handwriting and took it for granted the letter was for him. Picking it up, he saw that it was addressed to someone else and in a language he couldn't understand. Silhouettes on the walls of the room, or held within the book's pages. Wind catchers had been raised from the flat roofs. I was awoken by car horns and the incessant slamming of doors, later by a helicopter overhead. A white shape, too briefly at the window.

> a tent in stone
> or catafalque
> sculpted waves
> a blind man's
> -----------------
> palm against palm
> the hand inscribed
> the appearances
> moving across

A plank was positioned upright against the wall; next door, where he now slept, a ladder stood in the corner. The television left on in the darkened room. ...*wandering a maze of stone-laid alleys*, he wrote: *one house of black wood pressed tight against another.*

Blue and yellow lights in the dark, as the ship sailed towards the harbor. Searching, he said, *for a benediction.* She had covered the windowpanes with Greek script, white. Looking out at a small courtyard in a downpour. He was unable to rest or to act: if he lay down, he would almost immediately have to get up again, and then lie down once more, only to feel forced to rise and move around yet again. Jumping from the window occurred to him as a release from his distress. — Don't you realise, he said, that I'm the most important avant-garde poet in the world? It was believed that their accomplishments of singing, drawing and reciting were derived from the spirits who possessed them. The bowls, upside down on the floor, were traps, magic inscriptions on their interiors. A large abandoned dovecote had been built into the exterior of the house. Fearing capsize: in a sailboat in a squall. Flowers drawn in dark blue over the poem about flowers, obliterating most of the words.

Disembarking in torrents of rain. Locked out of his flat, wandering or waiting in dark streets, telephoning friends. — ...my *intuition*, the mother said; and the little boy asked, Does it tickle when you feel it? I sat on the deck in the cold night wind; he stood at the railings and talked with the Greek priest on his way home. They were both gazing at the island in the distance, and the priest said: Your friend's writing — I would like to read it. A group of singers in red gowns. Driving for miles for solitude, arriving at a crowded beach: what else could we do than talk and argue? He asked his daughter to help him choose which paintings to send through the post as a gift. In flame-light by the sea. Through what occurs, you search for a face, you work with or against each detail, building upon or erasing aspects, images. The child picked up the piece of paper from the floor and began chewing it. In distress: the doorframe a refuge. We looked back at her sitting in the car on top of the hillside, and saw that she was in tears.

Waking to a bright, warm morning in the port, with men washing down cars and motorbikes across the street. A mail-boat on a stamp; an envelope addressed to someone *in the neighborhood of the spirit*. Despite a heavy cold, I went out in the rain to meet him when he phoned to say that he was lost. — My doctor advised me to take long walks, I told him, with old friends from far away. Birds singing loudly as I made my way to bed. From my friend's flat, I walked past a church and drop-in center, charity shops and outdoor stalls. The balcony door swings back and forth in the wind. It was only when the service was over, and she was standing with her back to me, that I was able to speak to her; she turned to face me, and wasn't the friend — loved and lost for years — I thought I'd recognised. False apprehensions: a form of constancy. I was staying in a caravan, beside a shack with most of the rooms derelict, wild kittens for company. During her parties she would play recordings of Gregorian chant. When we met for the last time, you told me you'd been working on a series depicting nearby buildings, abandoned or set for demolition.

He sat on a rock in the field, singing to the sheep. Another day, he sang Mahler to the trumpeting elephants in the zoo. As we drove through the gateway, a dog with a crippled back leg came out to meet us. Later we went down to a restaurant by the sea, sharing a meal of fish and octopus and drinking wine. *Fragments of plaster, some with reed impressions, suggested the remains of houses built of plant material* — palm fronds, he thought — *and plaster*. From the street below, the old actress could be seen standing at the mirror framed in lights, preparing for the evening performance. The boy's limbs now affected by the medication, he found that he could move only with difficulty; so his mother helped him to walk the short distance to the hospital. After a long night of drinking his friend returned home, and removed several eggs from the refrigerator for juggling. A single sandal-print impressed in the pavement, rapidly filling with rainwater. On the floor of his bedroom he had arranged his clothes in pile after pile.

Gulls, motionless on posts by the water's edge; one turned its head to look at you when you came near. He walked along the path by the estuary, small boats out in the distance. Waking in distress from a dream of a friend's death. Even the gargoyles defeated him in his attempts at depicting the edifice. It was *a map of heaven,* yet one he couldn't follow. Shadow or stain, unfolding beneath the table. His earliest book, never finished, was entitled *We Shall be Friends in Paradise.* A floor of crystal, *shot with blue and purple, and green.* As the train pulled out, the conductor announced that they would be going on to their destination *without stopping at any intermittent stations.* She had to sit on a tiny, brightly colored chair to address the children. After her talk, she gave them cherry tomatoes, which most of them spat out. The final, almost empty images. To look, to lose, to meet or be met, to disappear.

Spiritual Letters
(Series 4)

We took the path along the cliff, by the ruins of a lighthouse. Waiting for her to arrive, he leaned against the balcony rail for the breeze — drinking wine and gazing at the people in the street. In the dream, water seeped through the ceiling and ran down the walls. She barely acknowledged me — to my sorrow — when I passed her outside the bookshop. Later, after hours, I sat with the staff watching television, while she lay on a couch at the back. My friend and his wife and children all lit tapers at the small shrine. — Here, he said, light a candle for someone you're thinking of. She sang to him over the phone, My home isn't here, my home's in heaven; saying, how sad that is! Stray dogs sat near our table outside the restaurant, watching for scraps. When we left, they followed us through the town and all the way down the hill as far as his house. His friend led him up the steps to a sandal-maker's shop. — He slips one of his poems in with each pair of sandals, he said. Turning to look at her, I saw her turn over in sleep.

She sent me a drawing of a rose, inscribed with my birth date. Sitting in a bar, thinking that you might walk in — without any reason for thinking so. Everything else in the painting — from the landscape to the person's body — was considered background for the depiction of the face. He told me that his favorite book was *The Incoherence of the Incoherence*; I didn't believe him. A rose petal inside the folded sheet. You suggested that I lie back on the floor, and when I did, you leapt on top of me from the couch. — What did you expect, letting yourself look so vulnerable? She recalled the smell of brandy (and the small bottle the woman kept in her handbag), the constant smoking of cigarettes. — I'm heartbroken, you said in the message you left me; my cat has disappeared. Later you found the cat, shut inside one of your trunks. The woman sat on the ledge, dangling her legs and looking pensively after the removal van. *Dear,* you wrote, *how warm and consoled I feel, embraced by your concern, this crucial day of my life.* They came back into the room and found her lying on the wrapped and crated painting.

Glass walls reflecting traffic, other buildings, passers-by. Clouds, birds, paper blown in gusts. The woman walked along the street at night, playing a wooden slide-whistle. Already late, you wanted to stop at the florist's so we could buy chrysanthemums for my friends. A young man stood at the end of the train carriage and delivered a long, apologetic speech about being homeless. He didn't try to collect any money; instead, he rushed past the passengers, and began again in the next carriage. You left after photographing the two drawings; later that day someone took a picture of the artist naked to the waist, in front of the huge drawing of her own eyes. I awoke from a dream in which my friend was knocking on my bedroom door. An open umbrella had been placed upside down and filled with herbs from the field.

There were no images of gods in their house; therefore they were assumed to be godless. Sunlight on olive green water; sheets of paper floating near a small yellow boat. Her fingers traced the words incised on the candle. I took his hand to help him up the steps to the concert hall. — I've been in and out of hospital for months, he said; but I will not miss this performance. Pine needles embedded in the paint. When I looked in the doorway, she was dancing to thirties Swing, *One O'clock Jump*. Through the branches, we saw the blue neon light at the end of the pier, reflected in the dark river.

Trees and stones may have retained some trace of the passing; but he was the sole human witness. In the dream he stood before us, blocking the narrow pathway; a blue iris in his hand. Bright moonlight on the estuary below the hill. I had gone to her place to play music, taking clarinet and bass clarinet. Arriving, I found people with instruments, yet no one playing a note; and when I asked about this, I was ignored or rebuffed. — Come at once, she wrote, for your poor daughter has died; and from this time on she will be happy forever.

> grass clay roofs
> flame melting wax
> light mirrored a voice
> breath a dark cell

He picked up the dead bird in his small hands, thinking he might wish it into living again. His mother startled him, saying: Don't think you can bring it back to life; and he was shocked that she could tell his thoughts. In the square, strings of lights in the trees. Lost in the strange city, we were surprised to see a friend coming towards us; we stopped him and asked if he knew the way to the train station. — I certainly do, he said; I once lived here, in a white van. They shared a kiss before she ascended into the air. — It was a kite to fly in, she said, and it could live on the water.

Ribbon windows and lights reflected in the water; sleet suddenly falling. We sailed under bridges, past tugs and pleasure boats. Books and a carafe held the billowing tablecloth down. Standing together at the party, he told me how he'd used the song of a hermit thrush in one of his clarinet pieces. A little girl wandered over and asked him if he'd like a glass of water. We were reminded to wear something red to the Pentecost service.

> in tears half-light
> a cliff the sea
> steps going up
> and down in sleep
> reflected face
> chiaroscuro

I was woken from a few hours' sleep in my narrow room by a knocking at the door. I'd thought it must be the neighbor's child, and was astonished to find it was a friend from far away. We ate waffles with acacia honey and drank white wine. Shattered glass underfoot on the pavement. A shudder of arrival, boat bumping against pier. She'd written his name and a time on her hand. On another's hand, he saw a small cross in ink.

After climbing the mountain, he arrived at the monastery during a snowstorm, and was given hot gruel by the monks. A child's tent, decorated with cartoon characters, on the balcony. I dreamt I was sitting with a woman on the roof of a tall building; birds were flying overhead, and I became giddy as they swooped lower and lower. You stood at the railings, watching the man in a skiff row past the pier. Tower blocks, barges, cranes, posts, reflected and blurred in the water. Coming home late at night, he saw the dwarf he'd noticed before in the neighborhood. She was stumbling around drunkenly, cigarette in hand; and he felt ashamed that he failed to offer any help. The spiritual body was said to be of *the fine celestial substance of light as it is native to the stars*. They were enjoined never to cut marks into their bodies because of the dead. Wandering into the unfamiliar temple, he thought he recognised a fellow believer, yet the more they conversed about religious practices, the more puzzled he became. We'd walked down the darkened street towards the café, past the high stone wall with hanging vines, the hill surmounted with trees, the house with a glass brick façade. After hearing us speak his own language, the man at the table across from ours had wine and food sent over, finally joining us for a drink. A swinging door and a bucket of blue paint: how many possibilities were there? — It was a void, she said; a *very interesting* void. The folded sheet of paper was thrown to the floor and stood.

You took me to a terrace overlooking the harbor, the sky darkening with rain clouds. On the doors were carvings of various figures, the faces scratched out. I sat down at a table and ordered a small abstract painting and an omelet. If I learned more of the language, I thought, I could order something different next time. — Don't gesticulate so much, he said as we stood in the parking lot; you might be mistaken for a gang member and get shot by a rival gang. The sign in the library read: Keep the Door Close at All Times. Shelves stacked with books, recordings, boxes of manuscripts. — Oh, she was really sweet, you said, but she was always drunk. Hanging from a board outside the station: a Missing poster, the image so weather-damaged as to be useless. He became convinced that his psychotherapist was a witch; however, she was clearly appalled when he told her. They found numerous shards of black porcelain bowls, some bearing inscriptions. An oil lamp the only light. *The house*, he'd written, *suffers on a journey.*

She was eighteen, she told us, when an elderly woman — once a famous Rembetika singer — tried to pick her up. Standing in front of the large office building, the tramp drunkenly ran his hands over the textured façade, delight in his face. You'd called in the early hours, forgetting the difference in time, and been acutely embarrassed. *I even miss the skirl of starlings in Leicester Square in the evening.* As the taxi turned into the lane, he noticed two teenagers embracing against a tree. Further down, several youths were lounging by a wall; the driver stopped to ask for directions to the guesthouse.

fallible
fall in a dance
eyes the wings
the dark sky

Old, torn posters in layers, where her shop had been, the building boarded up. Did she write it was a *mending rain*, or *unending rain*? He was helping his neighbor, a poet and retired rancher, to make a door for his front entrance. On the flat roofs: grass growing; pools of water. He said he didn't have another glass, and that I should cup my hands for the wine. When I'd finished playing the solo, she asked if there were any words to the music. To her surprise, I said that the song began *We all believe in one true God....*

It was a necessity, he wrote, that *the whiteness of their nature* should be restored. A blue and red bench between palm trees on the station platform. Waking in the tomb, covered in pus and blood, he remembered fucking his dead wife in his drunkenness. Remorse and sorrow overwhelmed him. He found himself back in the country — the very city — of his birth. After taking a tram a long way, he walked down to the beach; it was so crowded, he had to leap or vault over couples and groups. Turning on a light in the kitchen, I saw in a flash the bulb shatter, fragments flying across the room. — What would you do if you were still composing? — Well, there's a chord in one of my pieces that I think I'd remove. *I would eat rotten apples or dried-up pears if God would place them before me. Where the Word of God is, there is spiritual eating.* — Do you have any plates? she asked. — Why, do you want to break them? After visiting the library, we went on to a shopping center, then to a park where you persuaded me to join you on a child's slide. During the private view she spat on a handkerchief to clean one of the paintings.

             palaces
             of light sun
             moon a tent
             in the sky
             ----

palm-leaf book
----
torch-light or
candlelight
the black black
rectangle

We sat facing the glass wall, talking and drinking whisky, while coyotes howled in the distance. Earlier, we'd startled a roadrunner, skittish and quick, near a neighbor's house. When she was on her deathbed, I asked if I could kiss her forehead and she said yes. A room so small as to disappear. *A flutter or flicker*, he wrote, *could it be that there's nothing else?* He also wrote: *I've written about art, written about art... and always as more than aesthetics could include.* Brocade dress, draped over a chair; white lace curtain at the window. A past lover's face suddenly seen in a crowded post office, where she wasn't; a friend's face glimpsed in the Strand, shortly before his death in a distant country. We gathered in the garden while the minister pressed five nails into the paschal candle, which she then lit. When he asked me for a text, I began to work old drafts and notes into a new piece of writing. Face in memory or in dream: quiddity, exilic. He took a long walk alone, deep into the night. Dark trees, dark ground. *The spiral staircase in this house just reminds me of you*, he wrote to her. — Lollygagging is out of the question, you said. Hurried evacuations, fearful, desperate... with whatever belongings they could throw onto a wheelbarrow or a child's cart or else carry. Through a public garden, then down the riverside path — we opened the gate and walked over the ramp to where the houseboat was moored. Derelict boats in the mud; trees and houses on the other side of the river. As he left the carriage, the drunk suddenly spat in the face of a young woman who sat talking with her friend. The trumpet player stared out of a dark balcony in her dream.

a room
stranded
abandoned

She said she wished to *brush away the knocking on the door*. Visiting a friend once, he looked at a field of grass behind the house and thought: I could spend years drawing this and nothing else.... Of course, it wasn't true. It was said that their letters had been used to make cardboard boxes in Mexico City. In the opening of the story, a detective arrives in Athens from England, following a lead; he stands in a busy street, listening to a blind accordion player.... I failed to write any more; I tried to find the pages again and failed. The cat had died, he told her, and he'd keep it in the fridge until she returned from her holiday. – Gold is difficult... or doubtful. We'd been instructed to wash our hands before entering the room and after we left. After his wife's death he went through her diaries, crossing out passage after passage. *The only differentiations I could see were between very light and very dark tones, there was no green or blue or what have you. ...towards the end I was hallucinating and all sorts of strange things were occurring.* – He sang that song about footprints showing the way he'd traveled; don't you remember?

He ended up, late at night, drinking in a basement bar with five dwarfs, cast members of a show. You sat on the verandah, out of the afternoon sun, and smoked a cigar, nonchalantly stirring a martini with the arm of your sunglasses. — A strange holiday, she'd remarked, you sitting in the spare office and scribbling. She managed to trick the little Navajo boy into looking into her eyes. — I shouldn't have done that, she said, but he was so sweet — I just couldn't resist. ...*suddenly there was an explosion and ten feet in front of me I saw that a big tree had just been split by lightning. It was especially surprising since it wasn't raining, I hadn't seen any lightning or heard any thunder, it was simply overcast.* Returning to the hotel room late at night, he pulled back the coverlet on his bed and found that the sheets were stained with blood. A blond wig underneath the opposite seat in the train carriage. On the way to meet my friends for the first time, she asked me to go into a chemist's with her to buy nail polish, and we sat on a bench outside while she painted her nails. — She fell from the window; then the dogs tore her body apart. — No, she was *pushed.* Turning the corner, I came upon a building appalling in its absurd conglomeration of blocks and cylinders and reflecting walls. Along the sides, see-through lifts carried passengers up and down the main structure. Persistently denigrating, a father's words to his small daughter as they walk along the street. The architect made every attempt in his design to prevent students from attaching picture-hooks or nails to their walls. . . .*the being flitting about there among the shadows and flashes of light belongs to the unreal world.*

        silhouettes
        mirrorings
        waves of silk
        lit glass floor
        consumed she
        disappears
        into dark

He just didn't write enough music. He painted watercolors for forty years.... Cherry blossom and weeping willow by the lake's edge; birds splashing in the water. A girl sat on the grass, writing sideways in a notebook. — I must phone you to get that chord; I forgot to write it down. — Actually, it was two chords. When it became known that the country was under occupation, he went to the national library to renew his ticket. Sprinkling holy water over places she sensed as troubled; lighting candles for those she saw in dreams and visions as needing her help. She remembered a thousand people by name in her prayers each day. *Some of the copyists were prisoners-of-war or political hostages and worked in chains.* You told me you thought St. Paul was a landscape painter, not a tent maker. The church's ceiling, supported by pillars made from ships' masts, had been painted cream, and decorated in grey-blue and gold. Candles, sleeping bags and cushions on the floor. You'd added these words to the drawing: a greeting for Christmas, and an inscription in Greek (which I couldn't decipher). *It was my little cell of solid black.* Messages on slips of paper, thrown into a bowl and burned out in the garden.

Spiritual Letters
(Series 5)

The woman twice shouted hello, and I stopped twice in the dark street and turned and replied, Yes? — Wrong man, she said after a pause. She woke from a dream in which her father offered to have sex with her — woke, too, to the memory of his death. In the window of the children's hospital: papier-mâché figures of a cockerel and a mutilated man (one leg cut off at the knee). I turned down a lane past a silent and dark playground, slides and wheels only dimly visible. Met by chance in the street, she called for me to keep up with her as she ran down a flight of stone steps. I called back that I couldn't, as a bus had recently injured my foot. A metal ramp, leading to the long pier illumined by fluorescent light. I sat in the wine bar until three in the morning with an English friend back from Abu Dhabi and an African princess. The princess had held out her hand for me to kiss, but my lips met the long sleeve of her thick white wool cardigan. Branches hanging over the stone wall beside a bus shelter, a wooden bench further along the street. A night of strolling together, talking, waiting, leaving each other and coming back. A white china teapot, left on the edge of the footpath. She quickly had a thousand umbrellas bought and distributed, one for each person, when a sudden downpour interrupted the unveiling of the shrine. Was she really just trying to impress, or, as it was said, putting on airs? I thought she'd said *a lake of stone*, but later realised it was *a lake of snow.* — Let me in, your friend said, having woken you with his unexpected arrival, and make me some lasagne — then I'm back to work on my new masterpiece, which you'll read about in the art journals. He was carried by chair through the streets, with hundreds of helpers bearing his gold streamers.

the drawings
through crystals
frost snow hail
----
a candle
the mirror
sfumato

Gazing at his reflection, he mentally undressed himself; he couldn't linger, however, as his next analysand awaited him. While my sister tried out perfumes, I bought candied kumquats in another part of the shop. A girl in her mid-teens — my own age — by accident smeared my coat with her ice cream cone and apologised profusely. Bluish zinc cladding on the rooftops. She had scratched out her own eyes in the graduation photograph. — I won't be making the trip to meet you, I said; I've broken a rib. — Oh, she said, I know how painful that is; I once had several broken ribs... a spinal fracture... and facial lacerations. The architect suffered a fatal heart attack in a station lavatory, his body remaining unidentified for three days. Keeping three separate households, he'd deleted the address in his passport. Looking down from the top of the slope, to the slate roofs dissolving into the sea. Estuarine memories, dreams. As he lay naked in bed, an eagle smashed through the window of his hotel room and fell stunned amongst the glass fragments on the floor. Wrapping it in a towel, he threw the reviving bird back outside, where it flew off. He wrote to me of a lucid dream in which he swam above an underwater town and decided to dive down and explore, even going into some of the houses.

Yellow flowers, green leaves growing from no visible soil on a low roof across the way. Though they were staying at the same hotel, she sent her companion a series of postcards. On New Year's eve, we strolled among the crowds by the river, strangers shaking our hands or kissing us. He wrote of her performance that it belonged *more to pyrotechnics than to the art of dance. It is a sort of living fire-works.* Where he stopped the car at a light, a clarinetist was playing wildly and well, so that I wanted to get out and join in. You closed the wooden shutters and secured them each time before we left your apartment. *All in one day you get beautiful sunlight, thunder & lightning, wind & rain. Nights you look up at a clear, starry sky, and far off at no great distance hear thunder.* Shops and cafés; steps and public squares, old houses and fountains; walls with graffiti. At night, we walked so many streets, always.... — The bar was so dark you could scarcely see around you, but there was nothing to see anyway — no pool table, no pictures on the walls; the bar staff didn't try to talk to you, just poured drinks: it was my idea of paradise. He listened to his visitors' stories during the day, and to their dream-like stories at night. *Ah, if I die on the boat,* she sang, *throw me into the sea, / So that the black fish and salt water can eat me....* — Are you sure you're all right? he kept asking as we made our way back, drunk, on the bus, and I told him he was being condescending and finally stopped speaking to him. As soon as I entered my doorway, I collapsed to the floor. The monkey-puzzle I'd passed so often: uprooted, gone. The woman with a cane sitting in the train carriage, who looked so like you... could I really no longer tell? *Heartache, heartbreak: you old twin standards.* A few seats away from me, a man repeatedly called someone a bitch over his mobile, before he hung up. When she phoned back, he said: What do I want? I want to destroy your face. — There's a pigeon out in the garden that desperately tries to get into the church. — Perhaps it wants to be saved. *The love we bear to the blessed martyrs causes us,* he wrote, *I know not how, to desire to see in the heavenly kingdom the marks of the wounds which they received for the name of Christ....* Through the streets of the town or village, the funeral portraits were carried in procession with the bodies of the dead. Painted in black: words enjoining the dead to be happy, and a brief farewell. They'd accepted him as a novice in a Carthusian monastery, but he hadn't yet told them about the AIDS. In hospital, dying, the artist referred to the writing of his will as a "career move". *Another night I can't sleep,* he wrote in his diary, . . . *not even calling you to mind, your eyes, your hands, your mouth. . . yet unable to sleep because of you.* Alone in a small village, far from home — sudden anguish caught him, anguish building on anguish, and none of those he phoned responding to his calls. The group of friends went out together at the same date each year to repaint a small, neglected island church. It would have been impossible to get them to do it at some other time, simply for a filmmaker. *The day we were in the stocks I had this vision: I saw the place, which I had beheld dark before, now luminous; and my brother, with his body very clean and well clad, refreshing himself, and instead of his wound a scar only. I awoke, and I knew he was relieved from his pain.* He'd seen you running, pell-mell, down a crowded street. — I needed to get to a park bench to sit and think, you later explained.

On the way up the mountain to the monastery, we stopped at a café for some wine and listened to Rembetika on the radio. Nearby, at a street vendor's stall, she bought worry beads as a gift for me. He refused to ever return to the city of his youth – the only city where he'd felt at home – because of the atrocities the people had committed in wartime. Standing there in the streaming rain, you drew the attention of every passer-by to the place where a plaque to your favourite writer had once been. Balusters, laths, miter-joints and wainscots from demolished or abandoned buildings, stacked in boxes, on floors, or against walls. A rose window, the glass entirely a single blue. The opening of his exhibition had to be cancelled when the employees of the museum went on strike. Their demonstration caused an enormous traffic jam, and he admitted that he found the event extremely enjoyable – some people, indeed, accused him of arranging it. He wrote to me of his plans to build a labyrinth for children on one of the hills of Jerusalem. To reach the shops to buy bread, mild cheese, butter, sausage and wine, I walked up a steep slope and returned down it, always pausing to look out over the bay. A rock garden, with solar lights in a row; a smaller expanse of pebbles directly behind it. A rippling sheet of blue water beyond the back garden, green hills in the distance; the blue turning to silver, the hills darkening. She hid presents for the little girl behind the trees and in the bushes.

After the pub had closed for the afternoon, we wandered around trying to find more to drink and failed. — Manna from heaven! he exclaimed when we found a friend had left a bottle of rum on my doorstep. They hold wreaths of red flowers and glass cups, turning their heads at the sound of a familiar voice. In Reykjavik you bought a music box: to your surprise, raven cries came from it. *Our Lady, who appears in the stains and shadows of the subway.* He phoned from a hotel room in Cairo, leaving a message that he was dying. At his request they removed the altar and pews, and veiled the artworks and windows; robes, chalice and wine all had to be white, and the wafers bleached. As he sat writing, a sudden wind blew the sheet of paper from the table to the other side of the garden. The wooden skeleton of a building, enveloped in flames.

A small distance from the temple ruins we sat for a while and ate figs from a tree. By day or in early evening, children run amongst the jets of water, squealing, splashing, laughing; later, the fountain's still, the children gone. He changed the design for the labyrinth *from a square to a circle and finally to a triangle, the greater part... to be built underground.* Despite the late hour, a few figures could be seen in the elevator capsules, gliding up and down the side of the grandiose building, lit by blue neon. An empty can rattling along the road in a gust of wind. During the long wait for blood samples to be taken, I was curious about the other patients, but only made brief eye contact with anyone. Afterwards I decided to sit and read for a while over coffee — even if the poems happened to be about going blind or dying. *I am overcome with amazement when I hear a voice speaking in the wood, a hand raised to strike, the body bending over, raising itself, sitting down....* A wooden image of the goddess, removed, now lost; miniature statues of young girls and boys, her devotees, arranged in rows. They talked and talked about the problem of painting a white egg on a white tablecloth. Votive offerings, retrieved from the spring: dolls, toys, jewelry boxes, mirrors. To build the Christian basilica, they uncovered and carried off material from the ancient sanctuary, damaged by floods, across the valley. You described it for me: a miniature house, made of iron, placed on the bare floorboards. A tiny iron chair, also mere inches tall, nearby. No stained glass, no Agony in the Garden or Last Judgment: just seven windows divided into small clear panes. On the ceiling, gold flowers arranged in straight lines and circles, and gold rectangles. He got out of bed in the night, feeling ill, and fell on the stairs and lay there helplessly, with no one in earshot, and died. We wandered through the snow in the cemetery until we found the old Cabbalist's grave, surrounded by broken glass. Later that afternoon, in another cemetery, we saw the graves of writers and artists, snow falling faster, heavier. *Darkened windows, candle-light and battery torches, sirens and the army on every corner....* — Where did you think your friends had disappeared to, he asked, when they never called or answered your calls again? The woman still denied knowing about the deportations and deaths, angering him further. *I saw a ladder of tremendous height made of bronze, reaching all the way to the heavens, but it was so narrow that only one person could climb up at a time. To the two sides were fastened all sorts of iron instruments, as swords, lances, hooks, and knives; so that if any one went up carelessly he was in great danger of having his flesh torn....* She dreamt that she was eating curds, and woke with a sweet taste still on her tongue. *I at once told this to my brother, and we realized that we would have to suffer, and that from now on we would no longer have any hope in this life.*

Late one night, he began wandering unfamiliar back streets: and continued on and on, traveling enormous distances, even crossing oceans; though he only ever remembered walking. Far distant family and old friends met him on his way. Suddenly, a flock of ducks flew directly over my head, quacking loudly, as they swooped down towards the lake. Sitting outside a café, we talked about his child: four years old, she still couldn't talk, nor walk – small for her age, she was carried, or wheeled in a pram. They'd arrived at Giza in the evening, going straight to the pyramids from their hotel; but the noise of the crowd, then the bright images, lights and amplified voices made the child scream, over and again. Forced out of art school for his small, highly realistic images of buildings when large abstract paintings were obligatory, he later studied the history of architecture. – I survived my exams with the aid of a water flask filled with vodka, he told me. Printed on your postcard, with a schematic drawing of a person: *I'm lost.* After driving through the desert for a day, we stayed at a Navajo hotel, the only non-Indians there, with stray dogs roaming outside and a scorpion in our bathroom. The following afternoon we reached a lake with snow, water running over rocks, and trees in leaf. A diamond setter in the daytime, he played violin at night in the clubs along Eighth Avenue, amongst other expatriates. This night, the door's left open: for the passer-by, the wanderer, the erring traveler. After she'd taken me on a brief tour of the neighborhood, we went back to her house, where I met her husband; but something, it struck me, seemed wrong between them. She went out to smoke a small cigar; I took a walk and then a taxi ride, slowly realising how large and strange the city was... and I wondered about leaving. Fountains and pools, even a man-made lake, had been incorporated into the architectural complexes. Stone dragons, red and dark blue railings, trees in blossom. Within the temple, three rooms full of stacked small wooden tablets, recording in Chinese the names of the dead, their districts and villages. *She knew so much of the plants and birds and beasts around her, and loved the beautiful views over the sea of blue forest and real sea beyond....* Falling ill at a friend's, he stayed for a few days to recuperate. One afternoon they took a walk together, with one of his friend's daughters and the family dog: up a muddy hillside, then past frangipanis, ferns, eucalyptus trees. — Sister, let's go in, he said; they'd gone for a walk, and had been drawn by the sight of the basilica's spires. Years later, he could recall the ascension window's blues and reds, but not the cathedral gold windows; what she remembered, he would never know. He was taken aback during a sermon when his minister claimed she'd once glimpsed a ghost. As we left the station, we were caught up in a crowd surging towards the fireworks; even after the display, it was impossible for some while to disentangle ourselves. Two of the bridges had been closed off, and when we eventually reached a third and found it open, we were separated by the crowd and forced to go different ways. *I often wonder if you miss your clarinet. Sometimes I see young people in Bourke Street playing and think of you; there are a lot of buskers in the city these days, sometimes so close together that it is just a meaningless din.* I found myself staying back at the old family home, now my sister's, and sinking into despondency at the windows that were falling in, the front door not locking, and she refusing to do anything to fix them. *Dear adopted sister... thy history would furnish materials for one of the most interesting pernicious novels.* You accused her of bribing a surgeon to operate on you as a child, so that you'd be left with a cleft palate. Doors in the floor and ceiling, or opening onto blank walls; a reservoir of water over a fireplace; a staircase ending at the ceiling. When we were children, we had a cockatoo, a rosella and a crow, as well as dogs, cats and budgerigars. The cockatoo terrified us, and seemed to delight in it, chasing us around the yard while we screamed. Hearing me leave my room during the night, he covered himself in a sheet and hid in a closet to wait for my return. When he heard my footsteps, he opened the closet door, lifted his arms and walked towards me. *...she is just outside the door raving at me. Unfortunately she is involving other people... she is making me out to be a monster.* Returning from the hospital, she found that her daughter had taken all her cats to a shelter for strays. The journey led through a mountainous region, where a dragon lived near a lake; if it was not propitiated, it would cause storms of snow, hail, wind. His efforts at proselytising were hindered by the interpreter appointed to him, alcoholic and uncooperative. *There were two monastery buildings, but no monks lived in them. If a guest monk attempted to stay, the native people would drive him out with fire.* A hospital famous for its eye clinic: in a place where blind pilgrims once prayed to be cured. You wrote about the quality of the white in her paintings, which she brought back from distant travels: to Japan, Egypt, India, Java, Australia.... But it was her predilection for red — for painting red flowers — that I noticed. *...then we went on, and soon entered the region of the doum palm. Birds also became more common, we had seen troops of pelicans, ibex, storks, and ducks, and now we had abundance of larks and water-wagtails, and lovely long-tailed green birds almost like parakeets, but smaller.* She'd boiled water in an old black saucepan, and we drank tea together at a table made from a door. Across the street, my neighbors take turns sitting by the window, and smoking; their room's dark, apart from the bright, shifting colors of the TV screen. *Let the country with barbarous customs and smoking blood change into one where the people eat vegetables; and let the state where men kill be transformed into a kingdom where good works are encouraged.* Many of the vagrants he went to interview had never seen anything like his bulky tape recorder and often mistook it for a musical instrument, thinking at first he was a busker. ...*he took my hand, and we began to go through rugged and winding places. At last with much breathing hard we came to the amphitheatre, and he led me into the midst of the arena.* — Ah, you extraordinary illusionist! What have you come to show us this time with your occult arts? *Then out came an Egyptian against me, of vicious appearance, together with his seconds, to fight with me. But another beautiful troop of young men declared for me, and anointed me with oil for the combat.* He told his students that there were some things seemingly impossible to write about, such as his recurring dream of a mysterious route by which he traveled to see his mother, after meeting dear, long absent friends again. He would wake elated, and then remember that those he'd found once more in the dream were all dead. *In some cases a laurel crown in gilt, symbolizing their future happy state, has been added to portraits of both men and women....* The composer said that birdsong was "God's language"; he also affirmed the resurrection of the dead. The philosopher praised birdsong for its beauty, nothing more; while his religious philosophy, with its God who was forever in a state of becoming, had no room for any afterlife. *With these Eyes the cathedral's face is on the watch for the candelabra of heaven and the darkness of Lethe.* — Lines from your writing have been appearing in my dreams. *Often when I can't sleep at night I wonder what you are doing, trying to picture you*

89

and your pursuits. Vespers are said here, and sung; Bach is played, jazz, too. *Suffice to say there has been taken out of our limited garden one of the most perfect plants that ever was planted in mutability....* Long after her death, he depicted his granddaughter in his final painting — a little girl amongst the animals of the Peaceable Kingdom, leopard, lion, sheep, wolf and ox. We played music, recited, sang to my mother's memory. — I like your shirt, I said, conscious that I'd never seen him wear one before; he admitted that it was his girlfriend's, worn specially for the occasion. Walking by the lake, the trees illumined from below by yellow lights in the grass, he listened to the calls of the terns, cormorants, teals, mallards and grebes. *Thy rose bush is very pretty and thy geranium will be beautiful.* From the rooftop or windows, *we enjoy every fleeting glimpse of spring growing in the park, or a grey sheet of rain advancing over the trees. For flowers are good both for the living,* he wrote, *and the dead.* Beneath their feet: sun, moon and stars, and the signs of the zodiac, in the mosaic pavement. She wanted to go to the riverside to view the fireworks, and I went along to keep her company. The exploding lights that seemed to fall towards me and the booming noises brought on a panic attack, and I tried to leave; but the display ended, and I was caught in a dense, slowly moving crowd in the near-dark, and kept thinking I'd fall down. He smashed at the door of the synagogue with an axe until they let him in; taking a scroll from the Ark in his arms, he sang an ancient Castilian love song. At midnight, he rose from his bed and walked down to the sea, where he immersed himself according to a ritual. You sat every day by your dying friend's bedside, in accord with his wish. *It was*, you wrote, *a painful, a difficult death.* We were ordered into the sea by the sports master, and I was swept beyond my depth in no time; he called to me to swim back; and I called out that I couldn't, and then went under. I'd gone under three times, into a black tunnel of water, before two of the boys reached me. He collapsed in a tube train and was taken on a stretcher to street level; but he claimed to be all right and attempted to get up, and died of a heart attack. You walked to the hospital in a winter evening's severe wind; and then lost yourself in the mostly deserted corridors, before eventually finding the ward. Your friend was sitting on the side of the bed, and you sat down beside him and listened to his obsessive recital of mistakes and missed opportunities. — *I am praying to God,* he said, *but not to yours: to Osiris, Osiris.* Every evening he prepared a meal, and always insisted, much later, on making a pudding — often after a good deal to drink. He would reject each one after a single taste, and throw it into the garden: for the birds to eat, he'd say. It had been a half-hearted, absurd attempt at suicide, an outburst of adolescent despair in which you'd forced yourself to drink disinfectant as if poison; however, the doctor insisted your mother should have you hospitalised. She asked you what you wanted, and then accordingly told him: No. Having spent the afternoon writing in cafés and searching amongst bookstalls, he headed towards home; reaching it, he realised it was no longer where he resided, but his home of many years ago. Confused, increasingly desperate, he asked passers-by to help him: for he no longer knew at all where he lived. After eating and drinking on the beach with friends at night, he decided, against their advice, to swim along the coast and cast a long string of fishing hooks. He never returned; his corpse was discovered the next morning. A forest of ancient chestnut trees, brooks everywhere, and wild goats gazing intensely at you. He enjoyed the company of sponge divers, the poorest of all — but he was also friends with the captains of the boats. He had to be carried from the ship and taken to an abbey where he was known to the monks, who nursed him until he was strong enough to continue the journey. From the harbor, yellow lights shine in the distance; fishing-tackle hanging from a white T-frame where he stops to rest, and white boats in the water. Muffled voices and faint music from a larger boat, in an otherwise still night. When it began raining, I turned to follow the path back again; the estuary and the island out in the distance were only dimly visible through the rainy mist. When he switched on the kitchen light, something darted across the worktop and ran towards the wall: it turned around, finding itself cornered; and he found himself looking at a field mouse, which sat looking back at him. Another night, he stayed up reading in the lounge and listening to the storm outside; the mouse suddenly scooted across the floor in front of him and dove under the gas fire. Testing for a detached retina, the doctor put drops into my eyes to dilate the pupils. Afterwards, I attempted to walk home, but had to keep to the shadows to avoid being blinded by the sunlight, even then struggling to see, and having to stop. *He could hear the rivers protest as they were soiled by dirt washed into them, and could see blood seeping from the flesh of freshly cut fruits and vegetables.* Late in the evening, heavy rain beats and pours at the windowpanes, while I sit drinking wine. Earlier: a helicopter circling overhead repeatedly; and the sound of breaking glass in the street. *The raft went in out of the bright moonlight to pitch darkness, the roof of the cave so low that it seemed to be touching the top of the mast. Then, in the blackness, the rain and wind struck.*

Notes:

I began writing 'Spiritual Letters' in October 1995. The "letters" are an ongoing project of which five series have been completed to date.

I gave a talk entitled "Concerning 'Spiritual Letters'" at St James's Church, Piccadilly (London) in May 1998, later printed in 'Poetry Salzburg Review', No. 4, 2003, in which I stated:

"'Spiritual Letters' derives much of its inspiration from the Scriptures, especially from tracing certain keywords through the Scriptures using a Biblical concordance. [I stopped using the concordance after Series 4, as I felt that the process had become internalised, to a large extent.] One of the things that directed my approach was the Jewish Kabbalistic tradition, especially the 13th century work known as the 'Zohar' [by Moses de Léon]. I'd long been impressed with the 'Zohar's' mystical commentaries and elaboration upon Scripture, and its use of a creative, imaginative mode of interpretation involving independent narrative developments and rich and startling imagery. I was also impressed by the way the 'Zohar' moves far beyond the literal meaning of the Torah, in order to wrench free some more radical meaning.

"I'd also like to mention two other examples that I found very instructive — the work of two artists from the second half of [the twentieth] century. The first of these, Mathias Goeritz, was a wonderful sculptor, experimental architect and visual

poet. (...) I exchanged letters with him over a long period of time, and he was a great encouragement to me, especially when I was still a young poet. Mathias made a series of works called 'Messages' — a powerful series of abstract images, which he developed in response to specific Biblical passages, beginning around 1959 and extending through to at least 1975. This series was quite strongly in my mind when I began writing the 'Letters'.

"The other artist I want to mention is Wallace Berman. Berman was a Californian artist whose major works were created between 1964 and his death in 1976. In particular, he produced a long series of collages using a forerunner of the photocopier called a Verifax machine. These were in part inspired by his interest in Kabbalism, and combined a regular — yet variable — visual framework with a wide range of imagery (using images from popular culture and images derived from spiritual traditions, amongst other things). I was impressed by the way that Berman juxtaposed highly diverse images, as well as by the visual clarity of his work, however complex, and I was also very intrigued by his acknowledged inspiration from Jewish mysticism.

"I wouldn't see any direct influence from Berman on either the images or the way that the writing is structured in the 'Spiritual Letters'. Berman's significance for me was in the way that he provided a powerful example of a thoroughly contemporary art, which took inspiration from a religious or spiritual tradition. My own background is Christian rather than Jewish, but as I've already mentioned, I am also drawn to

Jewish mystical sources — so Berman's art seemed instructive and encouraging to me."

"So what I've been concerned with is a poetic form of writing — [mostly] in prose — that's in part determined by associations from specific Scriptural passages. But in common with the 'Zohar', 'Spiritual Letters' uses the Scriptures as "a springboard for the imagination" [Daniel Chanan Matt, Introduction to his translation of the 'Zohar', Paulist Press, 1983.] My writing sets up a relationship of sorts with Scripture and Scriptural commentary, but a very indirect one. (...) Also, my concern is with a writing that investigates and explores its themes and sources, never deriving from any sort of dogmatic position."

I'd tend to emphasise that, as I said in the talk, 'Spiritual Letters' "exists quite independently and possesses its own integrity and intensity", at the same time as it has a relationship to Scriptural tradition (however indirect).

I would like to acknowledge the sources of some brief quotations and paraphrases used in these writings, solely to give credit where credit is due. There is no reason for anyone to read these notes except out of curiosity.

In 'Spiritual Letters (Series 1)', the words "...may result in unexpected 'wipes' of color" are quoted from Philip Smith ("After Harry Smith" in 'American Magus: Harry Smith: A Modern Alchemist', ed. Paola Igliori, Inanout Press, 1996). The phrase "Dream geometry" derives from the title of an animated film by Canadian filmmaker, artist and poet Shelley McIntosh. "...as in a piece of arras work": Thomas De Quincey, writing about the way that music can provoke memory and indeed a sense of one's entire life. (I'm afraid I no longer remember which of his writings this occurs in.)

The first text in 'Spiritual Letters (Series 2)' uses a paraphrase from Robert Lax's 'Journal C' (a selection which I made from his journals and which was published by Pendo Verlag in 1990). For anyone interested, the passage occurs on p. 66, and begins: "i remember the people i loved (who have died) or who've just disappeared...." Bob Lax wrote to me on Dec. 14 1999 (the year before his death) that he was pleased about the paraphrase and that I should feel free to mention 'Journal C' or not, as I saw fit. The quotation "In a death, in weakness, inactivity, negation" is from Rowan Williams and was taken from Mark A. McIntosh's 'Mystical Theology: The Integrity of Spirituality and Theology' (Blackwell, 1998). "Bicycling through the city, with his ears painted red" is paraphrased from a biographical note in 'Paul Thek: The wonderful world that almost was' (Witte de With, 1995).

In Series 3, the sentence "Dear is the honie that is lickt out of thornes" is taken from Gerard's 'Herball'. "The motherfuckers won't let me sing" is supposed to have been said by Billie Holiday at Lester Young's funeral, though I don't remember where I heard or read this. "...wandering a maze of stone-laid alleys: one house of black wood pressed tight against another" is from my late friend Will Petersen's 'The Return' (privately printed, 1975). Will's autobiographical writings, as well as *his translations and his visual art, remain an inspiration to me. The artist Donald Evans was my source for the phrase "in the neighborhood of the spirit" (quoted in Willy Eisenhart, 'The World of Donald Evans', Harlin Quist, 1980). "Fragments of plaster..."*: *Mark Beech, "Fishing in the 'Ubaid: A Review of Fish-bone Assemblages from Early Prehistoric Coastal Settlements in the Arabian Gulf" ('The Journal of Oman Studies', Vol. 12, 2002). "...shot with blue and purple, and green"*: *quoted (from a 10ʰ century Irish source) in Jeffrey Burton Russell, 'A History of Heaven: The Singing Silence' (Princeton University Press, 1997).*

The fifth text in the third series is dedicated to the memory of Nicholas Zurbrugg, friend and fellow writer. The ninth text is dedicated to my late friend, the painter Lambros Koumantanos. The eleventh is dedicated to the poet Carl Rakosi, who was still alive when the text was written but has since passed away.

Series 4: "...the fine celestial substance of light as it is native to the stars" is from Wilhelm Bousset (trans. John E. Steely), quoted in Colleen McDannell and Bernhard Lang, 'Heaven: A History' (Yale UP, 2ⁿᵈ ed., 1988). "I even miss the skirl of starlings...": *a letter from a poet friend in Canada, clearly nostalgic for London. "We all believe in one true God..."*: *the Apostles' Creed, which Martin Luther set to music so beautifully. "...the whiteness of their nature"*: *from a Chinese Nestorian inscription, quoted in Richard C. Foltz, 'Religions of the Silk Road: Overland Trade and Cultural Exchange from Antiquity to the Fifteenth Century' (St. Martin's Griffin, 1999). (I've drawn upon Foltz's book in a number of instances in both this series and the next.)* "I would eat rotten apples...": Martin Luther, quoted in Eric W. Gritsch and Robert W. Jenson, 'Lutheranism: The Theological Movement and Its Confessional Writings' (Fortress Press, 1976). "The only differentiations I could see...": Ian McKeever, in an interview with Matthew Collings, 'Artscribe', no. 46, May-July 1984. "...suddenly there was an explosion...": John Levy, from an e-letter to the present writer. "...the being flitting about there among the shadows...": Loie Fuller, quoted in Richard Nelson Current and Marcia Ewig Current, 'Loie Fuller: Goddess of Light' (Northeastern University Press, 1997). "He just didn't write enough music": Morton Feldman ("Conversation between Morton Feldman and Walter Zimmerman", which I found at some point on the Internet, but which is now available in 'Morton Feldman says: interviews and lectures 1964-1987', ed. Chris Villars, Hyphen Press, 2006). "Some of the copyists...": Andrew George, in the Introduction to his translation of 'The Epic of Gilgamesh' (Penguin, 2000). "It was my little cell of solid black": Jay DeFeo, quoted in 'Jay DeFeo and The Rose', ed. Jane Green and Leah Levy (University of California Press, 2003). "– Come at once, she wrote..." is a paraphrase from a letter by a Roman Egyptian named Thaubas, quoted in Euphrosyne Doxiadis, 'The Mysterious Fayum Portraits: Faces from Ancient Egypt' (Thames & Hudson, 1995). "– It was a kite to fly in..." is paraphrased from Mabel Hubbard Bell (Alexander Graham Bell's wife), if I remember correctly – I don't remember the specific source. "I was woken from a few hours' sleep...": a paraphrase from Lisa Fittko, quoted in Momme Brodersen, 'Walter Benjamin:

A Biography', translated by Malcolm R. Green and Ingrida Ligers, edited by Martina Derviş (Verso, 1996).

In Series 5, #1, both the sentence beginning "She quickly had a thousand umbrellas bought...", and also the following sentence, were inspired by a passage in Rai Sanyō's "The Biography of Snowflake", translated by Burton Watson ('Anthology of Japanese Literature: Earliest Era to Mid-Nineteenth Century', compiled and edited by Donald Keene, Grove Press, 1955).

In Series 5, #2, "Yellow flowers, green leaves...": Robert Lax, in a letter to the present writer (from March 1994). Marcia Kelly, Bob Lax's niece and executor, kindly gave her blessing to my using this quotation and the following one by Lax. "...more to pyrotechnics than to the art of dance": a critic writing about Loie Fuller, quoted in 'Loie Fuller: Goddess of Light'. "All in one day...": Lax again, from a letter written in February 1995. "Ah, if I die on the boat...": from Gail Holst-Warhaft's translation of an anonymous Rembetika song, associated by many with Sotiria Bellou's great rendition. See Gail Holst (now Gail Holst-Warhaft), 'Road to Rembetika: music of a Greek sub-culture / songs of love, sorrow and hashish' (Denise Harvey, (1975) 1994). "The love we bear to the blessed martyrs...": St. Augustine, quoted in McDannell and Lang, 'Heaven: A History'. "The day we were in the stocks...": from 'The Passion (or Martyrdom) of Saints Perpetua and Felicitas' (the title is translated variously). I've used the translation by Rev. Alban Butler in this instance, from his book 'The Lives of the Fathers, Martyrs and Other

Principal Saints', Vol. 1 (D. & J. Sadlier, 1864).

In series 5, #4, "...from a square to a circle..." is taken from Michael Levin's introduction to 'Mathias Goeritz: architectural sculpture' (Israel Museum, 1980). "Darkened windows...": Momme Broderson, 'Walter Benjamin: A Biography'. "I saw a ladder...": 'Perpetua' again, using Butler's translation for the second sentence and Herbert Musurillo's (from 'The Acts of the Christian Martyrs', Clarendon Press, 1972) for the first. "I at once...": 'Perpetua', in Musurillo's translation.

With series 5, #5, many more voices have entered into the writing than with any other "letter", though of course it's also the longest of these texts to date. "She knew so much...": Marianne North, 'Recollections of a Happy Life', abridged by Graham Bateman as 'A Vision of Eden: The Life and Work of Marianne North' (Webb & Bower / Royal Botanical Gardens, 1980). "Dear adopted sister...": Edward Hicks, quoted in Alice Ford, 'Edward Hicks: Painter of the Peaceable Kingdom' (University of Pennsylvania Press, (1952) 1998). "Doors in the floor and ceiling...": paraphrased from "The House that Frank Built" by Dorothy G. Owens, on the website 'Old Spooky or Shangriold Spooky or Shangri-La' (about folk artist / architect James Franklin Butts). "There were two monastery buildings...": quoted in Richard C. Foltz, 'Religions of the Silk Road'. I've drawn upon Foltz's book for a few paraphrases in #5, as well. "...then we went on...": Marianne North, 'Recollections of a Happy Life'. "She'd boiled water...": this sentence is paraphrased from a passage in a letter from the poet Andrew Schelling to the present writer.

"Let the country...": from a Manichaean text quoted in Foltz's book (I've removed square brackets from "the country"). "...he took my hand...": 'Perpetua', in W.H. Shewring's translation ('The Passion of SS. Perpetua and Felicity MM. A new edition and translation...', Sheed & Ward, 1931, modernized by Paul Halsall on the Internet Medieval Source Book site). "— Ah, you extraordinary illusionist! What have you come to show us...": paraphrased from lines in the film 'Der Golem' by Paul Wegener (1920). "Then out came an Egyptian against me...": 'Perpetua', in the Musurillo and Butler translations (first and second sentence respectively). "In some cases a laurel crown...": A.F. Shore, 'Portrait Painting from Roman Egypt' (The Trustees of the British Museum, 1962). "With these Eyes...": Hugh of St. Victor, writing about Lincoln Cathedral (quoted in Painton Cowen, 'The Rose Window: Splendour and Symbol', Thames & Hudson, 2005). "Suffice to say...": Edward Hicks, quoted in Alice Ford, 'Edward Hicks: Painter of the Peaceable Kingdom'. (I've changed the spelling of "limmited" in the quotation to "limited".) "Thy rose bush is very pretty...": Sarah Hicks Parry, quoted in Alice Ford's book on Edward Hicks. "...we enjoy every fleeting glimpse...": Ben Sackheim, quoted in a memorial publication (2000) for Ben, who was a friend of mine. "For flowers are good...": Christopher Smart, 'Jubilate Agno', from a website provided by Ray Davis. "He smashed at the door...", and the next sentence, "At midnight he rose...", are paraphrased from passages in Gershom Scholem's 'Kabbalah' (Keter Publishing House, 1988). "I am praying to God...": Nicolas Berdyaev, quoting from a conversation with Vassili Rozanov ('Dream and Reality: An Essay in

Autobiography', tr. Katharine Lampert, Geoffrey Bles, 1950). "He could hear the rivers protest...": Zsuzsanne Gulácsi, on the prophet Mani ('Manichaean Art in Berlin Collections', Brepols, 2001). "The raft went in...": Ian Fairweather, quoted by Mary Eagle, "The Painter and the Raft", in 'Fairweather', ed. Murray Bail (Art & Australia Books / Queensland Art Gallery, 1994).

Series 5, #5 is dedicated to the memory of my dear friends Petros Bourgos, filmmaker and poet, and Michael Thorp, artist, poet and critic.

There are also a few other quotations and paraphrases in these "letters", which I haven't specified — either because I've forgotten the sources or because, in the case of personal correspondence, I prefer the sources to remain private.

D. M.
March 2010

About the Author

David Miller was born in Melbourne (Australia) in 1950, and has lived in London (England) since 1972. His recent publications include *The Waters of Marah* (Singing Horse Press, 2003 / Shearsman Books, 2005), *The Dorothy and Benno Stories* (Reality Street Editions, 2005), and *In the Shop of Nothing: New and Selected Poems* (Harbor Mountain Press, 2007). He has compiled *British Poetry Magazines 1914-2000: A History and Bibliography of 'Little Magazines'* (with Richard Price, The British Library, 2006) and edited *The Lariat and Other Writings* by Jaime de Angulo (Counterpoint, 2009). He has been working on the *Spiritual Letters* project since 1995. A double CD recording of David Miller reading *Spiritual Letters (Series 1-5)* is available from LARYNX (London).

Chax Press

Chax Press is a 501(c)(3) nonprofit organization, founded in 1984, that has published more than 120 books, including fine art editions and trade editions of literature and book art works.

For more information, please see our web site at *http://chax.org*

Chax Press is supported by individual contributions, and in part by the Tucson Pima Art Council and the Arizona Commission on the Arts, with funds from the State of Arizona and from the National Endowment for the Arts.